insomniac with a pen

kymberly krogh

BookLeaf Publishing

Presentation by *BookLeaf Publishing*

Web: www.bookleafpub.com

E-mail: info@bookleafpub.com

ISBN: 978-93-95413-12-1

First edition 2022

DEDICATION

to all the poems whispered to my bedroom ceiling in the moonlight. the sonnets i planned to "write down in the morning." you too, are a piece of me and, therefore, bear mentioning.

ACKNOWLEDGEMENT

momma, you have always supported this dream. josh and caleb, you cultivated my love of reading. to the rest of my family and friends, you love me through it all. thank you.

untitled

the irony of writing to forget
    lies
in the permanence of the ink

blank sheet

here and gone.
here and gone.
my cursor blinks her song
-a melody of my mediocrity-
disappointing even she,
the same untapped potential
as a fresh quill or pencil,
wasted.
for another day
i stare with nothing
left to say.
a timeless tune
taking another young writer
far too soon.

apologetically me

you asked who i am.

i never answered.

here's what i wish i could say:
i'm a fake smile,
false confidence,
and a hopeless romantic.

i'm hollow eyes,
a broken heart,
and a slave to pride.

but you wouldn't like who i am.

so i won't answer.

insomnia

it's hard to write
        when i'm
mostly active at night
        but so is my anxiety

drowning in
        my own
expectations

panic attacks
        my progress
while i continually
        digress deeper
into madness

untitled

5

i'm drowning in my own head,
in the sea of things left unsaid,
an ocean of dreams left for dead,
drowning, without ever leaving my bed.

low moaning siren

i'm drowning.
my body's drifting out to sea, and
the worst part is
i still hear you calling me.
your voice gently
rolls across the waves, and
crashes into my ears.
those hateful words sting
like the icy water
against my ravaged skin.
i float along
with no attempt
to resist your violent current.

sexual tension

hands nearly touching

with heavy breath
my lips fall open

i can't meet your gaze
wanting this moment to last
trapped in the
what-will-happen phase

tension vibrates through
the air as I meet your eyes

images flash through my mind

your hands tracing my thighs
lips and our whispered sighs

wild hair and glistening skin
losing ourselves to glorious sin

in this moment it's all possible
before anything becomes real

but soon we'll kiss
and break my daydream seal

lightning strikes again

i was up so late last night-
or early this morning
falling, for hours.
falling for you who i don't know
and maybe i don't want to.
something felt…different.
like maybe you could be the last first.

but the firsts are my high;
could your laugh be my new drug:
your smile, hands and space
between your arms?
or is my addiction to the new and safe
going to destroy what maybe
could be
my happiness.

i think
i'd like to try
to let myself
love you.

the bed's on fire

his indent smells of smoke,
strong enough to mask
the scent of their most recent sin.
her skin's still warm
from his last fleeting touch;
he's only been gone for moments
but he was there for less.
she drags the ashy aroma
deep into her lungs,
the memories sear into her mind-
images of tangled limbs,
sounds of ragged warm breath,
and the feeling of an inextinguishable flame.
she wants to burn forever;
but the sheets are already cold.

untitled

you like pretty lies.
so i'll hide my ugly truth,
hoping we survive.

another fallen angel

we all have our demons;
mine wears denim and
leather.

most would assume he stole my heart,
but all he did
was make me promise to keep it.

his sins are all my own;
i chase him with a shriveled,
barely beating organ
dripping between my
fingers.

with a crooked toothed grin
he traces the lines
he intends to break himself-

my demon finds the damage beautiful.

sometimes you have to become a monster to slay one

horns, claws and a thirst for blood
nothing he ever gave me resembled love

he scarred my body and dried my veins
hiding me away with rusted chains

but as i watched him i learned, studied
became what he was, my teeth got bloody

my horns were thicker and i grew wings
suddenly, he knew my fear and i was free

a prisoner i was no longer
but looking in the mirror
i still saw a monster

untitled

if the eyes are the windows to the soul,
perhaps the mascara-streaked glass
will conceal all that i wish to keep
                              hidden

it's not me, it's you

sexy does not amount to beautiful;
nor does fun mean dependable.

witty replaces the "apparent" lacking wisdom;
as mysterious belies an absence of vulnerability.

the things that they murmur
in their attempts to win me
are the same stinging insults
that my demons whisper each night.

i'm a trophy to be hung upon the mantle
after a night in the sheets-
a reminiscent story
swapped over five pm beers.

a night with me
earns a slap from the boys.

i dream of the day.
i dream of the man
who sees me as more than i've been labeled-
something worth holding onto
rather than a story to be told.

just a chance

oh, to be able to read a mind-
what secrets does that smirk hide?
with emerald eyes brighter than any moon
your voice's timber is my favorite tune.

raven hair and an ambiguous heart,
i've only known poisonous love
so i recognize the start.

untitled

17

if i could fall into your arms,
i would lie there until the sun faded into stars.
but you never catch me-

so i hit the floor,
a glutton for punishment once more.

reticent

don't cry
it ruins the lie
you feel nothing
another easy goodbye
you knew it would end
so don't pretend
swallow the tears
and smile

it's fine
your favorite line
even if it is
a defensive design

the darkest day in october

we ransacked your belongings that day
in a loving, inheritance sort of way.
i got the ring; she got your pearls,
broaches to each of the girls.
guests disappearing for private moments to
weep-
imagining their own grief more deep.
i took a sweater, covered in beads
and wear it many nights to sleep.
the sequins come off and it itches
but your smell is home, and I can
close my eyes and see you even though
i'm alone.

mourning after

foggy mornings
misty nights
thoughts of you
under twinkling lights.

heavy breathing
intertwining limbs
thoughts of you
touching my skin.

weeping trees
rippling sea
thoughts of you
caressing me.

but morning comes
and i'm alone
you're gone
turned back to stone.

untitled

21

day dreamscapes roll
across closed lids.
too tired to sleep.
lucid scenes,
memories and fantasies
twisted in the haze
of my subconscious gaze.

morning glory

come with me, my darling.
it's time to see the flowers bloom.
while many need the sun to grow,
a select few chose the moon.

they remind me of you, sweet child.
born among the tamed,
but meant to be wild.